Praise for
Real-Life Discipleship:
An Ordinary Man's Guide to Discplemaking

"The term "discipleship" is used routinely by churches worldwide to describe their commitment to help Christians grow spiritually. But only rarely do you find its practice being as rich and mature as what Tom Cheshire and Tom Gensler have described in *Real- Life Discipleship*.

Curriculum is important but the secret sauce to major life impact is found in their understanding and practice of one life impacting another's life. I recommend this book to anyone who wants to enhance one's spiritual pilgrimage with profound life transformation."

~Randy Pope,
Former Pastor, Perimeter Church, Atlanta, GA

"Tom Cheshire and Tom Gensler have learned firsthand how life-changing it can be to have the wisdom and guidance of a mature, godly man. Sadly enough, effective discipleship has gone by the wayside in many segments of the Church – but this vital, biblically mandated practice has the potential to change lives and transform families. I hope this compelling volume leads many men to consider how they are called to "do life" with other Christian men."

~Jim Daly,
President, Focus on the Family

"Most of us would agree that a disciple is 'one who follows Jesus'. Where we might disagree is how to make a disciple - how to make 'one who follows Jesus'. Tom Cheshire and Tom Gensler embrace the ministry philosophy of the Apostle Paul who did more than teach and encourage first century believers to follow Jesus, he instructed them to 'Follow me, as I follow Christ'. This model of I Corinthians 11:1 is the basis for 'Real Life Discipleship'. Grab this book and see what men following men who follow Jesus looks like in the twenty first century."

~Brian Doyle,
Founder and President Iron Sharpens Iron

"Finally, a book that does more than define discipleship. Cheshire and Gensler provide sound biblical teaching and engaging real-life stories that illustrate the truth they're presenting. If you're eager to grow as a disciple of Jesus and help other men grow along with you... this book is a must-read."

~Bill Perkins,
Author and Speaker

"Tom Gensler and Tom Cheshire are spiritual studs! These men walk the walk and talk the talk. Their new book puts down on paper what they have been modeling and teaching for years. It is a practical, Biblical and accessible primer for discipling men. Every local Church and every Pastor needs this tool in his own hands and in the hands of their men. God is raising up a generation of men who are servant-leaders for Christ and this new book by Tom Gensler and Tom Cheshire is helping it happen!"

~**JP Jones**,
Senior Pastor Crossline Church, author of *Facing Goliath*,
Radio Bible Teacher, "Truth that Changes Lives",
Adjunct Professor of Theology, Biola University, Men's Speaker, Iron Sharpens Iron Network

"Relational, intentional, strategic discipling, as illustrated in Tom and Tom's writing, is what Jesus' world-reaching church of the future must and will look like. Get on board asap!"

~**Hal Perkins**,
conference speaker and author of
Discipled by Jesus and *If Jesus Were a Parent*

"Tom Cheshire and Tom Gensler have done much more than just write an academic book on men's' discipleship. They have actually put down on paper a biblical, grace-filled, practical, sometimes messy guide for disciple making. Drawing from their own personal journeys as well as from their years of work in real life ministry with men, they have developed a tool that can help ordinary men step up and respond to Jesus' call to "go and make disciples."

~**Rick Caldwell**,
Director of Authentic Manhood and author of
33 the Series, A Man and His Marriage

"Jesus instructed us to go and make disciples, but in today's fast-paced world, it easy to put your head down, go through the motions and never have deep conversation or connection with another man. Tom and Tom have created a resource that can help men become the iron that strategically sharpens others. It is simple, short and practical."

~**Don Davis**, Retired NFL player
and Super Bowl Champion. Director of Football,
Pro Athletes Outreach

"I am excited that Tom Cheshire and Tom Gensler have provided us from their own lives how real life, practical discipleship works. I highly recommend you read their book."

~**Dr. Robert Lewis**,
Author and Founder of Men's Fraternity

"In over thirty years of ministry to men I have concluded that It takes a relational environment in order for truth to become transformational. Tom Cheshire and Tom Gensler have unpacked this idea brilliantly in *Real-Life Discipleship*. From the opening display of vulnerability and humility, to exposing the issues that hinder and bring men to passivity and the ultimate revealing of a practical plan, they help the reader discover Jesus simple model for real discipleship. A must read for every Pastor, leader and man who truly wants to grow and help other men do the same."

~**Vince D'Acchioli**,
Founder of On Target Ministries

"Let's cut to the chase. Show me HOW to do this crucial disciple-making work in the lives of men I know. Tom and Tom do this. They do it well in this book. Come on, men. This is HOW we can do this and do it well. Let's get it done."

~**Bruce W. Fong, ThM, PhD**,
Dean and Professor of Pastoral Ministries,
Dallas Theological Seminary Houston

"Deep and lasting change does not occur outside of transformational relationships; relationships that become the "life on life" context where the grace of the Gospel can confront our guilt and shame. Tom and Tom are not mere theorists. They live this. I am grateful for this highly practical tool that helps men take steps toward these kinds of intentional relationships."

~**Jeff Schulte**,
Founder & Executive Director of www.tinman.life

"What a gift! I believe this book is the answer to the question and the longing on the hearts of so many Christian men- 'what is a godly man and how do I become one?' Tom Cheshire and Tom Gensler not only tell us what it means to be a godly man but also compellingly show us how to become one. This book is a valuable resource!"

~**Dr. Crawford W. Loritts, Jr.**,
Author, Speaker, Sr. Pastor Fellowship Bible Church,
Roswell, Georgia

"Finally, someone has written a practical book about discipleship! God created men to lead other men to be like Christ. Unfortunately, few men have ever had someone show them how to lead other men. This book gives the basic building blocks that teach men how to lead other men to become more like Christ. Real Life Discipleship is written to help every man in the church to start living out the Great Commission."

~**Jeff Struecker,**
Retired Chaplain, formerly of the 75th Ranger Regiment

REAL-LIFE DISCPLESHIP GUIDE

The Ordinary Man's Guide to Disciplemaking

TOM CHESHIRE
TOM GENSLER

Made for Success Publishing
P.O. Box 1775 Issaquah, WA 98027
www.MadeForSuccessPublishing.com

Copyright © 2020 Tom Cheshire and Tom Gensler.
All rights reserved.

In accordance with the U.S. Copyright Act of 1976, the scanning, uploading, and electronic sharing of any part of this book without the permission of the publisher constitutes unlawful piracy and theft of the author's intellectual property. If you would like to use material from the book (other than for review purposes), prior written permission must be obtained by contacting the publisher at service@madeforsuccess.net.

All Scriptures are taken from THE HOLY BIBLE, ENGLISH STANDARD VERSION (ESV): ® Copyright© 2001 by Crossway, a publishing ministry of Good News Publishers. Used by permission. Thank you for your support of the author's rights.

Made for Grace is an imprint of Made for Success Publishing.

First Printing

Library of Congress Cataloging-in-Publication data

Cheshire, Tom and Gensler, Tom

Real-Life Discipleship Workbook: The Ordinary Man's Guide to Disciple-Making
p. cm.

ISBN: 978-1-64146-522-9 (Workbook)
ISBN: 978-1-64146-443-7(PBK)
ISBN: 978-1-64146-444-4 (eBooK)
ISBN: 978-1-64146-464-2 (Audiobook)
LCCN: 2019910828

Printed in the United States of America

For further information contact Made for Success Publishing
+14255266480 or email service@madeforsuccess.net

REAL-LIFE DISCIPLESHIP GUIDE

Battle Proven

*"No short cut exists for a deeper spiritual life...
the man who would know God must give time to him"*

— A.W. Tozer

How To Use This Guide	2
Introduction	3
Why Discipleship?	4
Real-Life Discipleship-SECTION ONE-SPIRITUAL FORMATION	7
BUILD THE RELATIONSHIP	9
SHARE YOUR FAITH	10
WHY WE ARE HERE	11
DEVELOPING SPIRITUAL DISCIPLINES	12
UNDERSTANDING AND READING THE BIBLE WITH A PLAN	13
PRAY WITH A PURPOSE	14
BUILD THE TEAM: PURPOSELY SURROUND YOURSELF WITH OTHER GODLY MEN	15
WORSHIPPING GOD	16
SERVANT LEADERSHIP IN THE BODY OF CHRIST	17
FRUIT OF THE SPIRIT	18
SHARE WHAT CHRIST HAS DONE IN YOUR LIFE	19
DEVELOP A GAME PLAN FOR SPIRITUAL GROWTH	20
TAKE A BREAK!	21
Real-Life Discipleship-SECTION TWO-THE MARRIAGE RELATIONSHIP	23
GOD'S DESIGN FOR MARRIAGE	25
SERVANT LEADERSHIP IN MARRIAGE	26
CHRIST AS THE EXAMPLE OF SERVANT LEADERSHIP	27
ROLES IN MARRIAGE	28
EXPECTATIONS FROM YOUR WIFE AND MEETING HER NEEDS	29
KNOWING YOUR WIFE'S LOVE LANGUAGE	30
COMMUNICATION AND CONFLICT	31
SEX AND PORNOGRAPHY	32
DEVELOP A GAME PLAN TO HONOR GOD IN YOUR MARRIAGE	33
TAKE A BREAK!	34
Real-Life Discipleship-SECTION THREE-FAMILY AND YOUR CHILDREN	35
WHAT KIND OF DAD DO YOU WANT TO BE	37
SUCCESSFUL FATHERING	38
WHAT YOUR CHILDREN NEED FROM YOU	39
DEVELOP A PLAN FOR FATHERING	40
TAKE A BREAK!	41
Real-Life Discipleship-SECTION FOUR-THE LOCAL CHURCH AND YOUR MANHOOD	43
HOW DO YOU FIT IN YOUR LOCAL CHURCH	45
BEING A PART OF THE SOLUTION, RATHER THAN THE PROBLEM!	46
BECOMING A SERVANT WITHIN YOUR LOCAL CHURCH	47
DEVELOP A GAME PLAN TO COMPLIMENT YOUR PASTOR AND STRENGTHEN YOUR CHURCH	48
TAKE A BREAK!	49

Real-Life Discipleship-SECTION FIVE-YOUR CAREER AND ITS IMPACT   51
YOUR VIEW OF WORK   53
GOD'S VIEW OF WORK   54
TAKING CHRIST INTO THE WORKPLACE   55
YOUR MANHOOD AND WORK   56
YOUR FINANCIAL STEWARDSHIP   57
DEVELOP A GAME PLAN TO WIN AT WORK AND HOME   58
TAKE A BREAK!   59

Real-Life Discipleship-SECTION SIX-WORKING A SUSTAINABLE GAME PLAN   60
REVISIT YOUR GAME PLAN FOR DEVELOPING SPIRITUAL DISCIPLINES   62
REVISIT YOUR GAME PLAN TO CREATE LASTING LOVE IN YOUR MARRIAGE   63
REVISIT YOUR GAME PLAN TO INVEST IN YOUR CHILDREN SO THEY MAY WALK WITH JESUS CHRIST   64
REVISIT YOUR GAME PLAN TO SERVE YOUR LOCAL CHURCH   65
REVISIT YOUR GAME PLAN TO BE A MAN OF GOD AT WORK   66
TAKE A BREAK! FAST AND PRAY THIS WEEK   67

Real-Life Discipleship-SCETION SEVEN-WHERE DO WE GO FROM HERE?   68
SO, HOW'S IT WORKING?   70
ROLES REVERSED   71
DISCUSS WHO'S NEXT   72
HOW DO YOU BECOME A MULTIPLIER?   73
PASSING THE BATON OF REAL-LIFE DISCPLESHIP   74
WATCH ME AS I LEAD   75

About the Authors   76

How To Use This Guide

The following pages are meant to be a guide providing you a topic, a scripture prompt to reflect on and help direct your conversation, and a set of example questions to help focus your conversation and time. There is a godly purpose for each section and conversation. There are times built in for rest, with each section having a specific purpose.

As godly men, we need to live our lives ordered by priorities, and this guide follows the way we strive to live our lives in Him.

- **Section One** is all about deepening your relationship with God
- **Section Two** is about strengthening your marriage
- **Section Three** is about being the best father possible
- **Section Four** is about your interaction in your local church
- **Section Five** is how you take your faith into the workplace
- **Section Six** is revisiting your plans for growth in these areas
- **Section Seven** is developing a plan to multiply and impact more men

This guide will not provide answers to every question. But, you are a man committed to advancing the kingdom of God, so be assured: when mistakes happen and failures occur, God's grace is sufficient for you. So press on, trust in Christ, do your best and invest in other men as other men invest in you.

Introduction

"What does it look like to disciple another man?"

Men have pondered this question for decades. They are wanting to help another man grow spiritually, yet have stopped short of becoming involved in disciple-making relationships because of fear of rejection, as well as not knowing what to do or where to start. This is not an exhaustive study on discipleship. Pastors and church leaders are often frustrated by the many offers of curriculums and resources that claim to help answer the question of "how to" disciple. Yet, in our experience, many give great information on why we should be discipling but fail to explain *how*. This is a practical guide to help the men of your church grow in Christ together and achieve the greater potential that God has for them. With the help of the Holy Spirit and our step-by-step approach on relevant topics, you will gain the know-how to achieve success and build godly relationships with the men of your local church.

We have personally witnessed the development of men who are better able to support their pastors and church leaders and strengthen their local Church. Through the years, we were discipled by many godly men. This guide is the result of what was learned through the Holy Spirit and those God-inspired men.

"...and what you have heard from me in the presence of many witnesses entrust to faithful men, who will be able to teach others also." 2 Timothy 2:2

Discipleship is not easy, and going the distance requires much perseverance. However, if you commit to digging deep together, you will sharpen each other, and your lives will be examples to lead others on this journey as well.

God bless you. Know that we are praying for you.

Sincerely,

Tom Cheshire & Tom Gensler

Why Discipleship?

Christ followers should be disciples... this we know. The biblical model for Christ-likeness is investing in men one-on-one in their day-to-day living. The great commission Matthew 28:18-20 gives us the command to make disciples.

Think about this for a moment: imagine a corporate CEO having employees unclear of what's expected of them. Every employer we have ever had, first indoctrinated us on the details of the company, safety concerns, and the how-to and goals of our employment to ensure the company success, as well as ours. Our first few weeks were spent close to someone assigned to train and mentor us. Secular businesses spend vast amounts of resources training employees. If this works for corporate America, why can't we apply this same principle in our churches?

We're taught discipleship from church podiums, and monthly men's breakfasts turn out about a dozen participants; however, this is not discipleship training. This has been largely ineffective to train leaders on the nuts and bolts in the how-to of mentoring men. We're producing pew-sitters who hear a great message, are entertained and feel good, then leave thinking they have fulfilled their Christian moral obligation for the week.

Just as a seasoned employee of a secular company takes the new employee under their wing, ensuring their success in the company, men of God need other men of God to become godly men. We also believe women need women to speak into them to understand biblical womanhood. Granted, small group ministries have had a more significant impact than the weekly messages from the podium, but this is still not the biblical model.

Discipleship is relational, life-on-life; a more mature person getting together with another on a regular basis to develop a relationship, exchanging information to the benefit of both, developing and growing in spiritual maturity. We contend for applying the Christ-model of growing in relationship with other men, speaking the Word of God into each other's lives, and deepening each other's practical application of the gospel in all of life's situations as Christ did with His chosen few. We believe that this is the right approach. Jesus selected twelve men with whom He spent quality one-on-one time; three with whom he dedicated much more personal time, and one particularly intimately. This is what we believe is the biblical model for discipleship.

Proverbs 27:17: "Iron sharpens iron, and one man sharpens another."

Titus 2:2-5: "Older men are to be sober-minded, dignified, self-controlled, sound in faith, in love, and in steadfastness. Older women likewise are to be reverent in behavior, not slanderers or slaves to much wine. They are to teach what is good, and so train the young women to love their husbands and children, to be self-controlled, pure, working at home, kind, and submissive to their own husbands, that the word of God may not be reviled."

Our focus is on discipling men. A man following God. A man who knows Him intimately and is becoming more Christ-like. A man who has a marriage and family, who has a genuine love and respect for his wife and wants to see his children become all that God wants them to be. A man who recognizes that his number one ministry is leading his wife and children closer to Christ, and does it each and every day—while going to work and working hard, demonstrating godly integrity and faith in Christ daily.

So, where are these men?

They're out there, but in limited numbers. Our heart's desire is to see armies of authentic gospel-centered men. We wake up every day desiring to see layers of discipleship taking place in local churches across America. By "layers" we mean that every man has a man discipling him, creating multi-generational investments in each other, all for the glory of Jesus Christ. Biblical manhood is in a state of confusion. For several generations, men have not had a clear vision of what biblical manhood looks like.

This is a guide intended to provide you with a relevant, practical, step-by-step approach to get involved in relationship with other men. This is *not* an exhaustive study on discipleship. There are plenty of resources available on this topic.

Discipleship is messy. Following this guide will likely also be messy, confusing at times, and difficult. You will be challenged. Turning away will sometimes seem like your best option, but you must resist those temptations. Christ called you to make disciples, and there are plenty of men who desperately want and need to be discipled. They don't act it, though. Just like us, they put on their church-face, but deep down, all followers of Jesus know they need a Christ-man friend in their lives. Christian men don't want failed jobs, marriages or estranged children. They are ripe for a win for their churches, communities, and our nation. They need men like us to depend on—to get in the game, persevere, and grow together in the knowledge of God and Christ-likeness.

> ***Matthew 28:19: "Go therefore and make disciples of all nations, baptizing them in the name of the Father and of the Son and of the Holy Spirit."***

You don't have to have a seminary degree or become a Bible scholar, have lived a perfect life or have all the answers. Were that true, none of us would qualify! That's why we all need Jesus. All we need now is a willing spirit to befriend another Christian man and grow together towards learning and applying deeper biblical truth in our lives.

> **We cannot change them; God does the changing... not us!**

We simply lead men to the written Word of God and help them apply that written word of God within the varying seasons of their lives. No one ever spent time with God and remained the same! Over the course of the next year, change will happen in God's timing. All it takes commitment, a willingness to invest into and grow together as followers of Jesus Christ.

> **Edmund Burke best revealed how Satan loves passivity: "The only thing necessary for the triumph of evil is for good men to do nothing."**

Section One

SPIRITUAL FORMATION

BUILD THE RELATIONSHIP
Hebrews 3:13

Bible verses to reflect on when building a relationship:
1 Corinthians 13:4-7, 1 Peter 3:8, 1 Peter 4:8, 1 Thessalonians 5:11, 1 John 4:11-12

Things to center your time around:
Meet and get to know each other. Create small talk, and simply learn about each other in great detail. You could spend weeks just getting to know each other in a very real and intimate way. Don't rush this process; discipleship is not a race.

Example questions:
Tell me about your dad.
Tell me about your wife.
Where did you grow up?
Tell me about your career.
Tell me about your children.
How long have you been married?

Notes from your time together:

SHARE YOUR FAITH
1 Peter 3:15

Bible verses to reflect on when discussing your faith experience:
Romans 12:2, 2 Corinthians 3:18, 2 Corinthians 5:17, John 6:40, Romans 10:5-13,
1 John 1:9, John 14:6, Hebrews 11:6, 1 Peter 1:8, Ephesians 2:4-5,8

Things to center your time around:
Faith Commitment: when did Jesus become real for you?
As the leader, begin by sharing your testimony and journey up to this point. It's important to clearly identify a faith commitment at some point, even if your follower hasn't grown much. If there is no clear faith commitment, then you need to share the gospel and introduce them to Christ. As the disciple-maker (leader), you need to model what a genuine and vibrant relationship with Jesus is and looks like.

Example questions:
Would you mind if I shared with you when I placed my faith in Christ?
Would you mind sharing with me when you placed your faith in Christ?
*(It's ok if they don't have an answer for this question... that's why you are doing this.
Encourage them and love them in this area and read through the scriptures referenced above.)*
Does your wife or girlfriend have a genuine, vibrant relationship with Jesus Christ?

Notes from your time together:

WHY WE ARE HERE

Matthew 28:18-20; 2 Timothy 2:2

Bible verses to reflect on when discussing where you are headed:

Proverbs 3:5-6, Romans 8:28, Ecclesiastes 3: 1-22, Jeremiah 1:5, Psalm 37:23

Things to center your time around:

Both of you should commit to meeting weekly for an extended period of time. We suggest committing to 1 year, for 1-1.5 hours per week. In our experience, this relationship needs to be clearly spelled out. Don't leave room for confusion on what is happening during your time together. As the leader, you are strategically and intentionally getting to know each other to help grow the gospel in the follower's life. Ensure expectations are communicated on both sides. Lay out where you are headed (if you choose to follow our guide) and see if there are areas that the follower would like to spend more time on then others.

Section One: Developing spiritual disciplines
Section Two: Examine the marriage relationship
Section Three: Examine the family, children and what does it mean to be the spiritual leader
Section Four: Discuss where the local church fits in with all this and a man's role in it
Section Five: Examine the career and how it is impacting their faith, family and church life
Section Six: Revisit your plans for growth in these areas
Section Seven: Develop a plan to multiply and impact more men

Example questions / statements:

What do you hope to get out of this?
Are you comfortable with where we are headed?
I hope to learn from you as you learn from what God has done in my life.
Do you understand Biblical discipleship? Can you explain your understanding?

Notes from your time together:

DEVELOPING SPIRITUAL DISCIPLINES

1 Timothy 4:7-8

Bible verses to reflect on when discussing where you are headed:
2 Timothy 2:15, 2 Timothy 3:16, 2 Timothy 4:2

Things to center your time around:
As the leader, discuss what it looks like to develop biblically rooted disciplines. Spiritual formation is the way to grow, and we must follow in the footsteps of Jesus Christ. Share with the follower ways that you have grown in Christ-likeness. Share with them what has worked for you and what has not. The point of developing spiritual disciplines is to drive men to God and His word, because that is where heart transformation happens—that leads to life change.

Remember: this should never be legalistic, but we do believe that doing things first out of duty for God can transform into a love and passion for obedience.

The Power of the 3 or P3

1. Understanding and reading the Bible with a **Plan** - Joshua 1:8
2. **Pray** with a purpose - 1 Thessalonians 5:16-18
3. **Purposely** align with godly men around you - Proverbs 11:14

Example questions:
What do you think would work for you?
Did you grow up around other godly people?
Do you have any regular spiritual disciplines?
Do you feel a desire to learn more about God?
Did you grow up reading the Bible and praying?

Notes from your time together:

UNDERSTANDING AND READING THE BIBLE WITH A PLAN

Joshua 1:8

Bible verses to reflect on when discussing where you are headed:
Joshua 3:9, Psalm 19:4, Mathew 4:4, John 1:1, John 1:14, 2 Timothy 3:15-16, Hebrews 4:12

Things to center your time around:

You can't use what you don't have, so the biggest step in discipling is developing a healthy biblical perspective. Properly understanding the Bible and what we believe about it is very important. As the leader, share ways that work to read the Bible consistently and thoroughly. We must drive ourselves and others to have an in-depth and intentional knowledge of the entire Bible. Ask the follower how they study the Bible. It's important to suggest some solid methods, but the point is to lovingly encourage the follower to understand that he needs to develop his own Bible study disciplines—not from a legalistic perspective, but a genuine love for the word of God because of the grace God has shown us (Romans 5:6-11). Part of your weekly meeting is accountability and understanding that developing spiritual disciplines is where growth takes place.

1. **Observation** – What is going on in the text? What sticks out? What do you learn about God from the text? What do you learn about man from this text?
2. **Interpretation** – What does the text mean? What is God saying/teaching in these verses? How should this text encourage you? Does the text warn you of anything?
3. **Application** – How should I apply what I read to my life? Is there anything I should do in light of what I read? Is there anything I should repent of?

Example questions:
Do you regularly read and study the Bible?
Did your family grow up studying the Bible?
Why is what we believe about the Bible important?
Why do you think it's hard to read and study the Bible daily?
Would it add value to your life as a man, husband, and father if you were daily engaged in God's word?

Notes from your time together:

PRAY WITH A PURPOSE
Matthew 26:41, Mark 1:35

Bible verses to reflect on when discussing where you are headed:
Luke 3:21-22, 1 Timothy 2:8, John 15:7, Philippians 4:6, Mark 11:24,
Romans 8:26, Matthew 6:6, Matt 6:9-13, John 17, Romans 1:10

Things to center your time around:
God reveals Himself to people as we pray. As the leader, you need the follower to understand that there is no right or wrong, but there are some "must be's" in this area. How do you have quiet time with God for personal reflection—time to collect yourself and your thoughts? Take time to explain that praying for their family and leading their wife and children in daily prayer before the Lord has to take place. The follower must understand leading in this area is his responsibility... not his wife or children.

Example questions:
How do you pray?
When do you pray?
What do you pray about?
Do you use a prayer journal?
What does your prayer life look like?
Do you pray with your wife and children?
How do you think you could develop a stronger prayer life?

Notes from your time together:

BUILD THE TEAM: PURPOSELY SURROUND YOURSELF WITH OTHER GODLY MEN

Proverbs 11:14

Bible verses to reflect on when discussing where you are headed:
Proverbs 27:17, Psalm 145:4, 2 Timothy 2:2, 1 Peter 5: 5-7, Proverbs 13:20, Hebrews 13:7

Things to center your time around:
The idea this week is to encourage the follower to have at least 3 men that he will regularly check in with over coffee, breakfast or lunch with the purpose of "Iron Sharpening Iron." As the leader, encourage him to give these men permission to speak into his life as they see fit. These should be men who genuinely care about him and want to see him personally healthy and spiritually strong.

A format we've learned to practice when meeting with another man is asking three simple questions.

1. How is your relationship with God?
2. How is your relationship with other believers?
3. How are you doing sharing Christ with a lost world?

It's called You're UP, You're IN, and You're OUT.

Example questions:
Have you ever had men in your life like this?
Do you have any reservations about being accountable to other godly Men?
Will you give me permission to lovingly praise and critique your life?

Notes from your time together?

WORSHIPPING GOD

Colossians 3:16

Bible verses to reflect on when discussing where you are headed:
Psalm 95:6, Isaiah 12:5, Luke 4:8, Psalm 95: 1-6, Psalm 96:9, Exodus 20:3, Ephesians 5:19

Things to center your time around:
The idea this week is to get the follower to understand that coming before the Lord and praising him for what He has done this week is important. It's important to convey that worship is not un-masculine and embarrassing. Spend some time talking about how important worship is in the life of a godly man. As the leader, convey setting the example of worship for his wife and children is a high priority.

Example questions:
What does your worship life look like?
Do you worship God with your wife and children as a family?
What are some ways you can increase worshiping God in your life?
What kind of music do you listen to when you're relaxing, driving in the car or on the computer?

Notes from your time together:

SERVANT LEADERSHIP IN THE BODY OF CHRIST

Mark 9:35

Bible verses to reflect on when discussing where you are headed:
1 Corinthians 11:3, James 3:1, Mark 10:42-45, Philippians 2:3,
Matt 20:25-28, Philippians 2:5-8, John 13: 3-5

Things to center your time around:
The idea this week is to define servant leadership in the body of Christ. There is confusion amongst many in our culture today. Success in the corporate world typically means you work long hours, step on others to get where you want, and only think of yourself. If we look at how Jesus defined leadership in the kingdom of God, he said things like "those who follow after me must be last, not first" and "the Son of man came here to serve, not be served." Encourage your follower that what works well in the business world typically does not work well in the body of Christ. Jesus' way is counter-culture, and we must live it the way He taught us.

Example questions:
How do you serve others in the body of Christ?
Do you volunteer at your local church; do you serve in other areas?
Explain to me your understanding of how Christ was a servant leader?
How can you apply servant leadership in your church, marriage, parenting and career?

Notes from your time together:

FRUIT OF THE SPIRIT
Galatians 5:22-23

Bible verses to reflect on when discussing where you are headed:
1 Corinthians 13:1-13, 1 John 2:1-29, James 2:1-26

Things to center your time around:
The idea this week is to get the follower thinking on the fruit of the spirit. What does it look like to examine qualities of a godly man's life such as love, joy, peace, patience, kindness, goodness, faithfulness, gentleness, and self-control? Spend some time this week going deeper in a few of these "must be's" that the follower thinks he struggles with. Fruit of the Spirit will grow out of Christ-likeness, not the other way around. Fruit is a byproduct of growth.

Example questions:
Do people see you as gentle?
Do others see the joy of Christ in you?
Do you have a peace about you that others would want?
Can people take you at your word? Does your yes, mean yes?
How are you loving your wife? Children? Extended family? Co-workers?
Do you have self-control with your eyes, mind, heart, appetite, and finances?
Do you demonstrate patience to your wife, children, family, friends, and co-workers?
Are you kind & good to those around you? Are you a faithful man in all areas of your life?

Notes from your time together:

SHARE WHAT CHRIST HAS DONE IN YOUR LIFE
Romans 12:2

Bible verses to reflect on when discussing where you are headed:
Ephesians 2:8-9, Colossians 3:12, Galatians 5:1, 1 Peter 2:16, Psalm 82:6, Isaiah 40:28

Things to center your time around:
The idea this week is to get the follower thinking of what God has been doing in his life. Think of how God has set you free and changed things within you. Reflect on how the Holy Spirit has brought about new awareness. Bring the follower to an understanding of being thankful. As the Leader, you might talk about what God has done in your life since you started meeting. If you have noticed growth in your follower, this is a great time to praise him and share how proud of him you are. There may not be big changes, but some change is better than no change!

Example questions:
How has God been working in our life?
What do you have to be thankful for lately?
Do your wife and family notice any changes in you?
Share with me something good this past week that God has done.

Homework for next week & follow up from previous weeks:
Remember, as the leader you must be living these topics out, as well as holding the follower accountable on a regular basis. This can be done by lovingly asking how they are doing in developing their core spiritual disciplines of reading the bible with a plan, praying with a purpose, and purposely surrounding themselves with godly men to encourage them, as well as lovingly rebuke them if necessary. Heart transformation will only happen if the follower is in the word of God, on his knees seeking God and being sharpened regularly by men of God. If he is not living out what you have discussed, ask questions. Have the things you've discussed been applied? If not, can you help him overcome? Celebrate the wins!

Come next week with a practical game plan that the follower believes he can follow. Write out action items that will keep him in the word, in prayer and surrounded by godly men!

Notes from your time together:

DEVELOP A GAME PLAN FOR SPIRITUAL GROWTH
Proverbs 14:23; 19:2

Bible verses to reflect on when discussing where you are headed:
Luke 14:28, Proverbs 16:3, Matt 6:33, Proverbs 19:21, Proverbs 16:9

Things to center your time around:
The idea this week is to get the follower thinking about working a sustainable, intentional plan that will lead to growth in Christ, his marriage, family, church and career. As the leader, you may want to show the follower what plan you work with and how it has helped you. There is no set way to plan and do this, but you should be able to work out something that is attainable for the follower.

Example plan:
I commit to reading my bible for how many minutes per day... follow a plan I found... I commit to spend time in prayer when... with my wife when... with my children when... I commit to spending time with other godly men when... they hold me accountable when... I commit to sharing my faith at work when... with my family when... with neighbors when...

Example questions:
Is this plan something that brings your wife and children into growing in the Lord as well?
So, what's your game plan? Is this something you can commit to over the course of your life?

Remember, we are not meeting next week, but there is homework. As the leader, encourage your follower to journal thoughts about his marriage—possible areas that need work, and a few things that he feels are going well. Refer to the next page for questions to help your follower think about his marriage.

Notes from your time together:

TAKE A BREAK!
We are not meeting this week.

Journal your thoughts on how your marriage is going.

A few questions for your wife:

- Ask your wife how she thinks your marriage is going?
- Does your wife see growth in you? If so, how?
- Ask your wife to share a few things that she thinks you need to work on.

Dreams for your marriage:

- Where would my wife and I like to be five years from now?
- How can God use our marriage to impact other marriages?
- Who can mentor my wife and me as a couple?

Section Two

THE MARRIAGE RELATIONSHIP

GOD'S DESIGN FOR MARRIAGE
Ephesians 5:22-33

Bible verses to reflect on when discussing where you are headed:
Genesis 1:27, Genesis 2:24, 1 Corinthians 7:1-40, Proverbs 18:22, 2 Corinthians 6:14, Psalm 85:10, 1 Corinthians 11:12, Luke 22: 25-27, Titus 2:4-5

Things to center your time around:
The idea this week is to take a closer look at marriage as defined by God in Ephesians chapter 5. This is the idea of co-equals in the eyes of God, created with different roles and responsibilities. This picture of marriage clearly identifies the husband as the head, but also as a servant leader, not a dictator or tyrant. As the leader, share about your courtship/dating, engagement and wedding.

You will be spending the next few weeks digging in on this topic, so take your time and really hash it out.

Example questions:
What is your perspective on marriage?
Growing up, what did you see from your parents' marriage?
What changes do you think you need to make in order to align with the word of God?
How do you think your marriage is going based on the homework you had from last week?

Notes from your time together:

SERVANT LEADERSHIP IN MARRIAGE
Ephesians 5:25

Bible verses to reflect on when discussing where you are headed:
Luke 22: 25-27, Titus 2:4-5, Genesis 1:27, Genesis 2:24, 1 Corinthians 7:1-40, Proverbs 18:22, 2 Corinthians 6:14, Psalm 85:10, 1 Corinthians 11:12 Genesis 2:20-23, Genesis 3:6

Things to center your time around:
The idea this week is to carry over your conversation from last week. Really dig into the idea of Ephesians 5:25. As the leader, use your own marriage successes and failures as an example.

Example questions:
Do you date your wife?
What does your marriage look like?
What do you believe about your wife's salvation?
What would your wife say your marriage looks like?
Would your wife say she knows you love and serve her?
How can you begin serving your wife like Christ served the Church?
Would you mind if I spoke with your wife via phone call to hear her perspective on your marriage?
Give me a few examples of other couples who have a relationship and marriage that you admire.
Give me some examples of ways you are continuing to grow in your marriage, i.e., books, studies, conferences.

Notes from your time together:

CHRIST AS THE EXAMPLE OF SERVANT LEADERSHIP
John 13:3-10

Bible verses to reflect on when discussing where you are headed:
John 13:12-15, Matthew 20: 25-28, Hebrews 13:7, Mark 9:35, 1 Peter 4:10, John 3:30, Mark 10:45

Things to center your time around:
The idea this week is to finish flushing out the topic of servant leadership. We have talked about servant leadership in marriage, and now we must continue examining servant leadership from Christ's perspective. The follower must understand that he is here to serve first in his marriage, then his family, then his church, then his career. You need to really hammer home the follower's marriage being a top priority—second only to his personal relationship with the Lord.

Priority list
1st my relationship with God (not to be confused with church service or works).
2nd my marriage, and how I lead by sacrificially serving my wife both in word and deed.
3rd my children, and how I love them and meet their needs while clearly communicating that their mother is still priority.
4th your obligation to lead in the local church (don't confuse this with your personal relationship with God).
5th your faith being lived out at work.

Example questions:
Are these priorities that you can live by?
Write down for me a list of your top priorities.
What changes do you think you need to make?

Notes from your time together:

ROLES IN MARRIAGE
(For Single Men To Aspire To)
Genesis 2:24

Bible verses to reflect on when discussing where you are headed:
Genesis 2:18, Galatians 3:28, Ephesians 5, James 1:19,
Proverbs 10:19, Ephesians 4:26, Matthew 5

Things to center your time around:
The idea this week is for the follower to really think about God's roles for marriage. In Genesis 2, God created man first and then created woman to be man's helper. Please ensure that the follower understands that a wife's role of helper to her husband does not give her less value in God's eyes (Galatians 3:28). We are created as co-equals in the kingdom of God with different strengths given to men and women. Ephesians 5:25 gives a tall order for husbands to love their wives like Christ loved the church—Christ died for his bride, the church! In light of this truth, help the follower understand that this is true servant leadership. Take some time and flush this out with your follower: what roles have he and his bride taken up in their marriage? i.e., he does outside work and she does inside work or whatever that may look like. Help him understand that no matter where they land, he needs to be loving. His leadership should be out of serving his wife with Christ being his example.

Example questions:
What gifts does your wife have?
What do you think you could do better?
What would your wife say about all this?
Do you mind if I talk with your wife about this topic?
What roles do you and your wife assume in your marriage?
Do you clearly understand Genesis 2, Galatians 3:28 and Ephesians 5?

Homework for next week:
Ask your follower to have both him and his wife go online to www.5lovelanguages.com and take the profile to identify how you give and receive love. This will likely cost you money, but is a part of growing in your faith and marriage and is important for you. We also recommend that you purchase and read the book together.

Notes from your time together:

EXPECTATIONS FROM YOUR WIFE AND MEETING HER NEEDS
1 Peter 3:7

Bible verses to reflect on when discussing where you are headed:
Mark 10:6-9, 1 Corinthians 7:3-5, Proverbs 5:18-19, 1 Corinthians 7:10, 1 Corinthians 7:5

Things to center your time around:
The idea this week is to help the follower understand that his needs likely won't be met if he is not diligently working to meet his wife's needs. You might have a frank discussion about whether or not his wife is meeting his needs sexually. Discuss how servant leadership and operating in proper roles translate into needs being met.

Example questions:
Can you list off your wife's top needs?
Do you feel like your needs are being met by your wife? Explain.
What does it mean for you to understand your wife (from 1 Peter 3:7)?
Do you think you have room for improvement in meeting your wife's needs?

Notes from your time together:

KNOWING YOUR WIFE'S LOVE LANGUAGE

Colossians 3:19

Bible verses to reflect on when discussing where you are headed:
Mark 10:6-9, 1 Peter 3, 1 Corinthians 13:4-13, 1 Corinthians 7:3-5, Proverbs 5:18-19, 1 Corinthians 7:10, 1 Corinthians 7:5, Genesis 2:18, Galatians 3:28, Ephesians 5, James 1:19, Proverbs 10:19, Ephesians 4:26, Matthew 5

Things to center your time around:
As the leader, make sure your follower understands what love languages are and how each of you in the marriage relationship give and receive love. He should have gone online and taken the 5 Love Languages Survey. The five love languages are Words of Affirmation, Acts of Service, Receiving Gifts, Quality Time & Physical Touch.

Example questions:
So, what's your love language? What's your wife's love language?
Do you think understanding yours and hers has helped you? In what way?
Do you have a grasp on the five love languages and how they apply to your marriage?
How do you plan to operate in your marriage with this new information you have been given?

Notes from your time together:

COMMUNICATION AND CONFLICT
Ephesians 4:25-29

Bible verses to reflect on when discussing where you are headed:
1 Corinthians 13, 1 Corinthians 7:1-40, Hebrews 13:4, Ephesians 5:21,
James 1:19, Mark 10:6-8, Luke 6:38, Philippians 4:13, Colossians 3:9; 19

Things to center your time around:
Conflict in marriage is inevitable. The idea this week is helping the follower understand the way he communicates with his wife lays a foundation for everything else. Conflict in marriage must not be done in a way that reflects culture, but in a way that reflects Christ and his written word. We must reject the ways of our world and follow Christ on this matter.

Example questions:
Do you fight to win?
Are you and your wife on the same page?
How do you communicate and fight in your household?
Would you mind if I contacted your wife on this matter?
What do you need help in concerning communication and conflict?

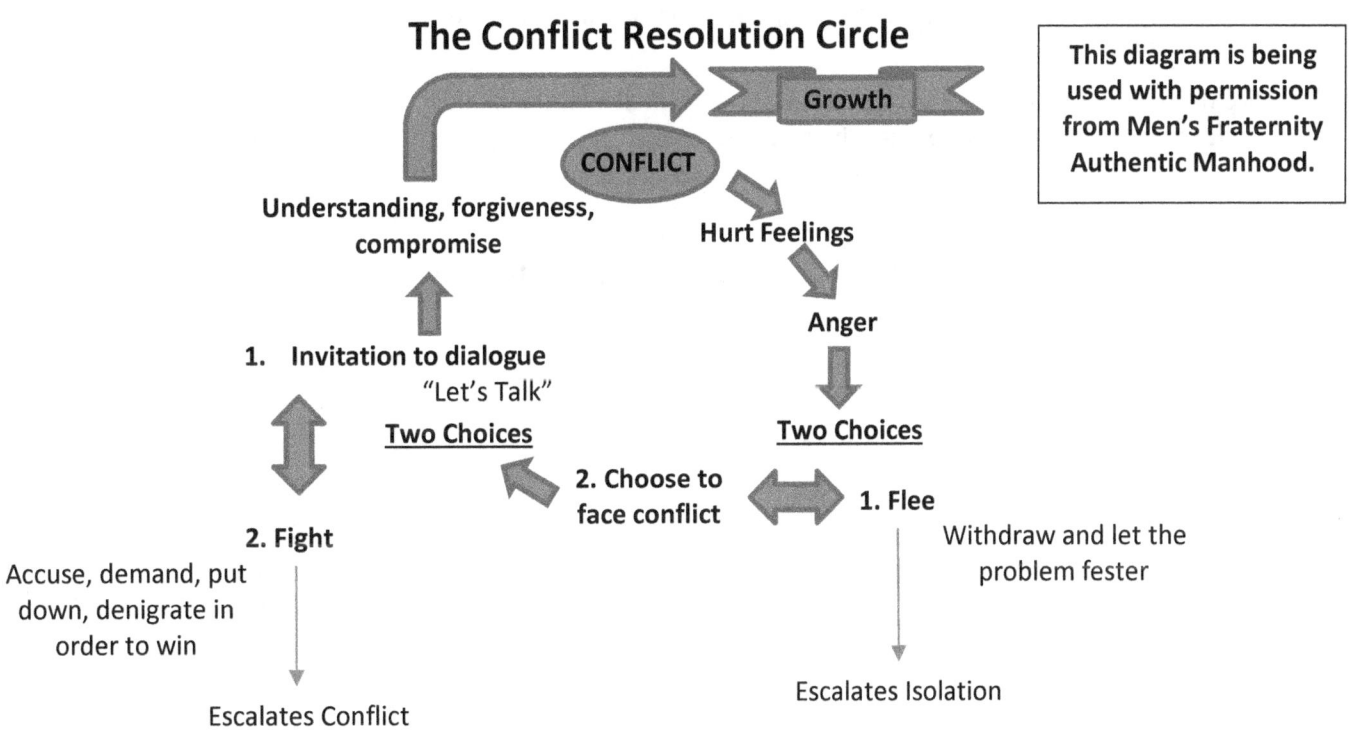

This diagram is being used with permission from Men's Fraternity Authentic Manhood.

SEX AND PORNOGRAPHY
Hebrews 13:4

Bible verses to reflect on when discussing where you are headed:
Genesis 39, 1 Corinthians 6:12-20, Ephesians 5:21, Proverbs 5:18, Colossians 5:19

Things to center your time around:
The idea this week is to help the follower understand God's perspective on sex. It is imperative that you as the leader model honest open transparency in this area. We suggest you touch on pornography, lust and masturbation. Men are struggling with these issues, and obviously they aren't going to go away during one discussion. However, honesty and accountability can help a man be transformed in this area. The follower must understand that a weekly sex drive is healthy and normal, and a good sex life has a lot to do with servant leadership, roles, communication and understanding love languages. All of these working for the glory of God will produce a happy healthy sex life between a husband and wife.

Example Questions:
How is your sex life?
Are you satisfied with your sex life?
How do you deal with lust and masturbation?
What does it look like to fight those temptations?
Honestly, tell me when you last looked at pornography?

We have accountability on every electronic device we own in the ministry. It's highly recommended that both of you sign up for accountability software with www.xxxchurch.com or www.covenanteyes.com. Signing up for accountability is a must be in the life of every Christian man.

Notes from your time together:

DEVELOP A GAME PLAN TO HONOR GOD IN YOUR MARRIAGE
The Song of Solomon 5

Bible verses to reflect on when discussing where you are headed:
Mark 10:6-9, 1 Peter 3, Proverbs 5:18-19, 1 Corinthians 7:5, Genesis 2:18, Galatians 3:28, Ephesians 5, James 1:19, Proverbs 10:19, Ephesians 4:26, Matthew 5, 1 Corinthians 13, 1 Corinthians 7:1-40, Hebrews 13:4, James 1:19, Mark 10:6-8, Luke 6:38, Philippians 4:13, Colossians 3:19

Things to center your time around:
The idea this week is as the leader to take all you have been talking about and develop an intentional and strategic plan to serve, love and lead our wives just like Christ does for his bride, the church. Take some time and identify where you are prone to be passive as a husband. Think long term and sacrificial!

Example questions:
Do you date your wife weekly?
How do you plan to serve, love and lead your wife daily and weekly?
How do you initiate in your marriage without your wife asking?
Do you and your wife pray together?
Do you study scripture together?
Does your wife see Christ in you?
Is there another married couple that could mentor you and your wife together?

<u>We are not meeting next week, so there is a little homework. Take your wife on a date and discuss what it would look like to pray together daily, read the bible daily, date weekly and what couple in your local church could mentor you in the area of your marriage.</u>

Notes from your time together:

TAKE A BREAK!
We are not meeting this week.

Homework for your week off:

Take your wife on a date and discuss what it would look like to pray together daily, read the bible daily, date weekly and what couple in your local church could mentor you in the area of your marriage?

Write your notes from your time with your wife and let's discuss next time we meet.

Section Three

FAMILY AND YOUR CHILDREN

WHAT KIND OF DAD DO YOU WANT TO BE
Psalm 127

Bible verses to reflect on when discussing where you are headed:
Psalm 139:13-16, Ephesians 6:1-3, Deuteronomy 6:6-9,
Proverbs 22:6, Ephesians 6:4, Colossians 3:21

Things to center your time around:
The idea this week is to get the follower thinking about how God would want him to raise his children. Something to focus on is the difference between how culture wants us to raise our children and how God wants us to raise our children. Help the follower identify where he is at and explain that it's not too late to make Christ-centered changes, no matter the age of his children. As the leader, you may want to revisit your follower's relationship with his own dad.

Example questions:
How can I help you in this area?
What kind of father do you think you are?
Do you think you have room for improvement? Explain.
What would your wife and children say about the father you are?
What kind of father do you think God wants you to be? Do you see these character traits in yourself?

Notes from your time together:

SUCCESSFUL FATHERING
Proverbs 29:15

Bible verses to reflect on when discussing where you are headed:
Proverbs 13:24, Proverbs 19:8, Proverbs 23:13-14, Proverbs 29:17

Things to center your time around:
The idea this week is to help the follower understand that no matter the age of his children, he can be an engaged and loving father who is leading his family towards Christ.

Example questions:
What would your wife say?
Do you pray with your children?
How do you lovingly discipline your children?
What areas do you think you can improve in?
Do you lead your children in worship and bible study?
Do you often lose your temper and get angry with your children? Can you improve in this area?
What is the primary purpose for discipline? Help children understand sin, temptation, and obedience.

Notes from your time together:

WHAT YOUR CHILDREN NEED FROM YOU
Matthew 17:5

Bible verses to reflect on when discussing where you are headed:
1 Kings 9:4, 2 Chronicles 17:3, 2 Chronicles 26:4, 2 Timothy 3:15,
Titus 2:4, Titus 2:6-7, Joshua 24:14-15, Deuteronomy 6:4-9

Things to center your time around:
The idea this week is for the follower to understand that his children need him and need to hear things from him. As he follows the example of Christ, Dad's example is tremendously important in the life of his children. It's never too late to engage your children in a relationship. Being present and available are two things you can do today that will make an impact.

No matter what their age, three things every child needs to hear from their parents are:
- I Love You
- I'm Proud of you
- You are so good at…

Example questions:
Do you have a weekly date with your children?
How can you spend more time with your children?
What areas can you improve in this area? How can I help you grow in this area?
What are your thoughts on the three things children of all ages need to hear from their father?

Notes from your time together:

DEVELOP A PLAN FOR FATHERING
Ephesians 2:10

Bible verses to reflect on when discussing where you are headed:
Psalm 139:13-16, Ephesians 6:1-3, Deuteronomy 6:6-9, Proverbs 22:6, Ephesians 6:4, Colossians 3:21, Proverbs 13:24, Proverbs 19:8, Proverbs 23:13-14, Proverbs 29:17, 1 Kings 9:4, 2 Chronicles 17:3, 2 Chronicles 26:4, 2 Timothy 3:15, Titus 2:4

Things to center your time around:
The idea this week is to help the follower develop an intentional and strategic long-term plan to win big as a dad. Help him understand that it's never too late to grow in this area.

Example questions:
How can I help you grow in this area?
So, what's your plan to grow as a father?
Do you see how God has made each child unique?
Does your work life interfere with you being a father?
Is it realistic to take your children on a date weekly? Why not?
Do your children know that your wife is more important to you than they are?
Give me some practical ideas that you can do this week to love your children more.

<u>We are taking a break next week, but there is homework. Take your children on a date next week with the time you would have spent meeting with me.</u>

Notes from your time together:

TAKE A BREAK!
We are not meeting this week.

Homework for your week off:
Take your children on a date during this week's break and take notes on how it went.

Notes on how your date went with each of your children:

Section Four

THE LOCAL CHURCH AND YOUR MANHOOD

HOW DO YOU FIT IN YOUR LOCAL CHURCH?
1 Corinthians 12

Bible verses to reflect on when discussing where you are headed:
Acts 20:28, Hebrews 13:17, 1 Peter 5:2, Acts 6:1-15, Titus 1:5-9,
Ephesians 4:12, Ephesians 5:29-30, Romans 12:5-8

Things to center your time around:
The idea this week is to help the follower understand where he fits within his local church body. Most men aren't leading well at home, in the workplace or at church. The follower must understand that all godly leadership starts at home in his marriage with his children. The home is the proving ground for all other leadership opportunities.

Example questions:
How could you serve your local church pastor?
Do you tithe to your local church? Do you support other ministries?
Do you think your local church could use your abilities for the glory of God?
Describe to me a servant leader at home. Describe to me a servant leader at church.
We have talked about servant leadership in your marriage and family, how is that going?

Notes from your time together:

BEING A PART OF THE SOLUTION, RATHER THAN THE PROBLEM!
Luke 7:1-10

Bible verses to reflect on when discussing where you are headed:
Matthew 12:36-37, Galatians 5:19-26, Proverbs 28:25, Galatians 5:15,
Romans 8:7, John 3:17-18, Ephesians 4:29

Things to center your time around:
The idea this week is to get the follower thinking about solving problems rather than creating them. It seems that so many people are church hopping these days, and they leave when they encounter a "problem" instead of staying and being apart of the solution. We look at church membership kind of like a marriage: you don't just walk out on your wife when you don't like something, and you shouldn't do that with your church either. Help the follower understand that he is under the authority of his pastor and his commitment to his local church body should be taken seriously.

Example questions:
How can I help you grow in this area?
How are things going at your church?
How can you be a part of the solution?
How do you view church membership?
Do you wish things would be different? How so?
Are you committed to your local church body for better or worse?
Do you and your wife have the same feelings on this topic? Why or Why Not?
Have you talked with church leadership about your involvement and ideas you may have?

Notes from your time together:

BECOMING A SERVANT WITHIN YOUR LOCAL CHURCH
Titus 1:5-10, 1 Timothy 3:1-13

Bible verses to reflect on when discussing where you are headed:
1 Timothy 3:1-16, Acts 20:28, Hebrews 13:17, 1 Peter 5:2, Acts 6:1-15

Things to center your time around:
The idea this week is to get the follower seriously considering how he can get involved in a role of some kind in his church. He needs to believe that he has value to add and that God desires him to lead well at home, church and in the workplace. Emphasize not seeking to be a leader, but to serve as Christ modeled to us. Ensure your follower understands his priorities need to be his personal relationship with God first, then his marriage, then his family, and then his local church. Men often will throw themselves into serving at church and completely miss that God, marriage and family should be of higher importance.

Example Questions:
What gifts do you possess?
What do you think you're good at?
How could you fill in gaps at your local church?
Have you talked with your pastor about serving him?
Are you able to lovingly serve and fill in gaps without becoming part of the problem?

Notes from your time together:

DEVELOP A GAME PLAN TO COMPLIMENT YOUR PASTOR AND STRENGTHEN YOUR CHURCH
Colossians 3:12-17

Bible verses to reflect on when discussing where you are headed:
Matthew 12:36-37, Galatians 5:19-26, Proverbs 28:25, Galatians 5:15, Romans 8:7, John 3:17-18, 1 Timothy 3:1-16, Acts 20:28, Hebrews 13:17, 1 Peter 5:2, Acts 6:1-15

Things to center your time around:
The idea this week is to help the follower develop an intentional and strategic long-term plan to serve within his local church.

Example Questions:
So, what is your plan?
How can I help you grow in this area?
Have you talked with your pastor yet?
Does your local church need your help?
What do you think you could do to help?

We are taking a break next week, but there is homework. I want you to set up a meeting with your pastor and ask how you can serve him.

Notes from your time together:

TAKE A BREAK!

We are not meeting this week.

Homework for your week off:

We are taking a break this week, but there is homework. I want you to set up a meeting with your pastor and ask how you can serve him.

Take notes below on how your meeting went and share next week.

Section Five

YOUR CAREER AND ITS IMPACT

YOUR VIEW OF WORK
Proverbs 16:3

Bible verses to reflect on when discussing where you are headed:
Colossians 3:22-24, John 6:27, 2 Thessalonians 3:10, Proverbs 14:23

Things to center your time around:
The idea this week is to get the follower thinking about how he views work. Does he think of work as a means to an end, or does he see it as a calling from God? Help him understand that a negative perspective on work is not of God.

Example questions:
How do you view work?
Do you like what you do?
What would be your dream job?
How can I help you grow in this area?
Do your co-workers know you are a believer in Jesus?

Notes from your time together:

GOD'S VIEW OF WORK
Ephesians 2:10

Bible verses to reflect on when discussing where you are headed:
1 Corinthians 10:31, 2 Timothy 2:15, Colossians 3:22-24, John 6:27,
2 Thessalonians 3:10, Proverbs 14:23, Genesis 2:15

Things to center your time around:
The idea this week is to get the follower thinking of work the way God does. Help him understand that God desires for him to win at both work and home. His work life is a very important part of his faith walk, and he will likely have many opportunities to share his faith with co-workers.

Example questions:
How could you change their view of you?
Do you think your co-workers see Christ in you? Why or why not?
Do you think you can serve God in your work environment? Why or why not?
Do you understand that God desires much more out of your work than you do?

Notes from your time together:

TAKING CHRIST INTO THE WORKPLACE
Matthew 5:13-16

Bible verses to reflect on when discussing where you are headed:
Matthew 5:13-16, Philippians 2:13, John 14:26; 16:13, Colossians 3:23-24,
Titus 2:9, 1 Peter 3:15, Ephesians 2:10, Matthew 28:19

Things to center your time around:
The idea this week is to get the follower thinking about living out their faith in Christ at work. All Christians are called to be salt and light, and we should be an example of Christ at work; being a Christian example at work is not just for "full-time Christian workers." Most men spend 1/3 of their life working, so help your follower understand that God has a much bigger plan for them than to just punch a clock and get a check.

Example Questions:
What does it look like to be a Christian at work?
Do your co-workers know that you are a Christian?
Do you have a plan to share the gospel at work with your co-workers?
What are a few things you could do to begin living out your faith at work?
What is something you can do to change the negative way people view you at work?

Notes from your time together:

YOUR MANHOOD AND WORK
Proverbs 22:1

Bible verses to reflect on when discussing where you are headed:
Proverbs 22:1, Proverbs 22:29, Proverbs 25:13, 1 Thessalonians 5:11, Ephesians 4:29, Matthew 5:37, Psalm 15:4, Proverbs 10:9, Proverbs 22:3, 1 Corinthians 6:18, Proverbs 6:32-33, Proverbs 7:10-12,15,21-23, Proverbs 6:25-27

Things to center your time around:
The idea this week is to get the follower thinking of his reputation at work. This is important, especially if your co-workers know you are a Christian. We are all called to be an example for Christ—how people view and know us at work may affect how others view our church and knowing Jesus Christ.

Example questions:
Do you demonstrate integrity at work?
So how do you think people view you at work?
How can you improve your reputation at work?
Have you stepped on others to get where you are at?
When you walk by a group of employees or co-workers, what do you think they say?
Have you ever asked some of your work friends what your reputation at work is like?
How do you handle your failures at work in a way that demonstrates humility and repentance?

Notes from your time together:

YOUR FINANCIAL STEWARDSHIP
Hebrews 13:5

Bible verses to reflect on when discussing where you are headed:
Hebrews 13:5, 1 Timothy 6:10, Proverbs 22:7, Ecclesiastes 5:10,
Proverbs 13:11; 13:22, Malachi 3:10, Luke 12:23-24, Acts 8:20

Things to center your time around:
The idea this week is to get the follower thinking about what they do with their finances. How does their pay affect their home life, their church life and their community? It's appropriate at this point to ask the follower whether they tithe to their local church or not. Are they generous with their finances in the community? What is the financial picture at home?

Example questions:
How can I help you improve in this area?
Do you mind if I ask whether you tithe or not?
Are you supportive of local things in our community?
Do you mind if I ask whether your finances at home are in order or not?
How do you use the money you earn at home, in your local church and the community we live in?

Notes from your time together:

DEVELOP A GAME PLAN TO WIN AT WORK AND HOME
2 Timothy 2:15

Bible verses to reflect on when discussing where you are headed:
1 Peter 3:7, Proverbs 22:6, Colossians 3:23-24

Things to center your time around:
The idea this week is to get the follower thinking about how they intend to win at both work and home. What are some things they need to be doing that they are not yet doing? Being a Christian example at home with their wife and children and then going to work and modeling out their faith to their co-workers is God's design.

Example questions:
What are some positive changes I can help you make?
Do you mind if I hold you accountable to these changes?
Have you developed a plan to ensure you are winning at both? How's that working?
Name three things you can do this week that will help you have success in this area?

We are taking a break next week!

Notes from your time together:

TAKE A BREAK!
We are not meeting this week.

Homework for your week off:

Take your wife on a date and discuss your career and it's impact on your marriage and family. Get honest feedback from your wife on how well you balance work and home.

Write your notes from your time with your wife and let's discuss next time we meet.

Section Six

WORKING A SUSTAINABLE GAME PLAN

REVISIT YOUR GAME PLAN FOR DEVELOPING SPIRITUAL DISCIPLINES
Proverbs 21:5

Bible verses to reflect on when discussing where you are headed:
Luke 14:28, Proverbs 16:3, Matthew 6:33, Proverbs 19:21, Proverbs 16:9

Things to center your time around:
The idea this week is to get the follower to revisit their sustainable game plan from the spiritual formation section. Unless we develop a plan and execute it with loving accountability, we are not likely to follow through with it.

Example questions:
Can I hold you accountable?
So, how are you doing with your spiritual disciplines?
What changes do you think you still need to make to continue growing?
Have you noticed a change in you since you committed to spending more time with the Lord?
Has your wife and family noticed any changes in you since you have committed to growing more?

Notes from your time together:

REVISIT YOUR GAME PLAN TO INVEST IN YOUR CHILDREN SO THEY MAY WALK WITH JESUS CHRIST
Deuteronomy 6:6-9

Bible verses to reflect on when discussing where you are headed:
Psalm 139:13-16, Ephesians 6:1-3, Proverbs 22:6, Ephesians 6:4, Colossians 3:21, Proverbs 13:24, Proverbs 19:8, Proverbs 23:13-14, Proverbs 29:17, 1 Kings 9:4, 2 Chronicles 17:3, 2 Chronicles 26:4, 2 Timothy 3:15, Titus 2:4

Things to center your time around:
The idea this week is to get the follower thinking about launching his children out into the world. What is he doing now that will invest into their future later? Teaching and instructing our children in the ways of the Lord should be the norm no matter their age.

Example questions:
Do you see Christ in your children?
Do your children see Christ in you?
What are you doing as a father to develop and grow your children closer to Christ?
What are some positive changes I can help you make? Can I hold you accountable?
Do you know whether your children have a personal relationship with Jesus Christ or not?

Notes from your time together:

REVISIT YOUR GAME PLAN TO CREATE LASTING LOVE IN YOUR MARRIAGE
1 Peter 3

Bible verses to reflect on when discussing where you are headed:
Mark 10:6-9, Proverbs 5:18-19, 1 Corinthians 7:5, Genesis 2:18, Galatians 3:28, Ephesians 5, James 1:19, Proverbs 10:19, Ephesians 4:26, Matthew 5, 1 Corinthians 13, 1 Corinthians 7:1-40, Hebrews 13:4, James 1:19, Mark 10:6-8, Luke 6:38, Philippians 4:13, Colossians 3:19

Things to center your time around:
The idea this week is to get the follower thinking about his marriage and how he can ensure it will go the distance. Marriage is forever and putting in work and investing in it should be the norm.

Example questions:
Do you date your wife weekly? Why not?
What are some things you wish would change about your marriage?
Is your marriage an example to your children for what it should look like?
Have you invested in your marriage with a conference or a nice trip lately?
If I were to call your wife today, what would she say about the state of your marriage?

Notes from your time together:

REVISIT YOUR GAME PLAN TO SERVE YOUR LOCAL CHURCH
Colossians 3:12-17

Bible verses to reflect on when discussing where you are headed:
Matthew 12:36-37, Galatians 5:19-26, Proverbs 28:25, Galatians 5:15, Romans 8:7, John 3:17-18, 1 Timothy 3:1-16, Acts 20:28, Hebrews 13:17, 1 Peter 5:2, Acts 6:1-15

Things to center your time around:
The idea this week is to get the follower thinking about how they are supporting and developing their local church and pastor. How are they part of the solution rather than the problem? Investing in our local church and the folks who attend church with us should be the norm.

Example questions:
Can your pastor count on you?
Does your local pastor know who you are?
Do you strive to bring unity to your church?
How can you become more involved in serving?
Do you approach your pastor with a servant's heart?
Have you become more involved with your local church since we started meeting?

Notes from your time together:

REVISIT YOUR GAME PLAN TO BE A MAN OF GOD AT WORK
Colossians 3:23

Bible verses to reflect on when discussing where you are headed:
1 Peter 3:7, Proverbs 22:6, 2 Timothy 2:15

Things to center your time around:
The idea this week is to get the follower thinking about their witness at work. Are they truly being the hands and feet of Jesus at work?

Example Questions:
Would your co-workers say you are a Christian?
So how are you doing sharing your faith at work?
What can I help you do better as far as sharing your faith at work? Can I hold you accountable?

We are taking a break next week!

Notes from your time together:

TAKE A BREAK!
FAST AND PRAY THIS WEEK

Section Seven

WHERE DO WE GO FROM HERE?

SO, HOW'S IT WORKING?
Proverbs 19:21

Bible verses to reflect on when discussing where you are headed:
Proverbs 21:5, Luke 14:28, Isaiah 32:8, Deuteronomy 28:1-68, 1 Corinthians 14:40, Proverbs 16:9

Things to center your time around:
The idea this week is to get the follower really focused on the disciplemaking process that you have been going through using this guide. He must understand that accountability is crucial in all of this and he must know that there are godly men who love him and want him to thrive in is faith, marriage, family and career.

Example questions:
Do you have a better understanding of what discipleship is now?
Have you seen spiritual growth since we have been meeting? Explain.
Are there any specific areas you feel we need to spend more time with?
Would you feel comfortable doing real-life discipleship with another man?

Notes from your time together:

ROLES REVERSED
2 Timothy 2:2

Bible verses to reflect on when discussing where you are headed:
Matthew 28:18-20, Matthew 5:14-16, Luke 14:27, Ephesians 4:11-17,
Luke 9:23, Luke 6:40, 1 Corinthians 11:1

Things to center your time around:
The idea this week is to get the follower thinking about leading someone else. Multiplication is the key here: you helped him grow and now the time is nearing that he will help someone grow, leaving you to find a new follower to help grow.

Example questions:
What do you think we could have done differently?
Are you interested in investing in another man? Why not?
What would you say about our time together the past year?

Notes from your time together:

DISCUSS WHO'S NEXT
Colossians 1:28-29

Bible verses to reflect on when discussing where you are headed:
Matthew 28:18-20, Matthew 5:14-16, Luke 14:27, Ephesians 4:11-17,
Luke 9:23, Luke 6:40, 1 Corinthians 11:1

Things to center your time around:
The idea this week is to get the follower thinking about who he is going to pray about approaching to enter into a real-life discipling relationship. You need to ensure the follower knows that we as men need to continue investing in other men. Men need men to become men!

Example questions:
Would you take your son through a process like this?
Is there a particular man you have in mind to pray about?
Do you think you have value to add to another man's life?

Notes from your time together:

HOW DO YOU BECOME A MULTIPLIER?
1 Corinthians 11:1

Bible verses to reflect on when discussing where you are headed:
Matthew 28:18-20, Matthew 5:14-16, Ephesians 4:11-17, Luke 6:40, Luke 9:23, Luke 14:27

Things to center your time around:
The idea this week is to get the follower thinking about how God wants him to invest in other men. He should want to help other men grow spiritually and be a part of a discipling culture in the local church. Communicate how important his role in all of this is and that he needs to not give up if it does not happen with the first guy he tries to disciple.

Example questions:
How can I be praying for you?
What are your fears in all of this?
So, have you decided on who you think God wants you to invest in?
What's your plan to approach him and ask him to pray about going on this journey with you?

Notes from your time together:

PASSING THE BATON OF REAL-LIFE DISCIPLESHIP
Matthew 10:16

Bible verses to reflect on when discussing where you are headed:
Matthew 28:18-20, Matthew 5:14-16, Ephesians 4:11-17,
Luke 9:23, Luke 6:40, Luke 14:27

Things to center your time around:
The idea this week is to get the follower and the new man he plans to disciple thinking about how this is going to work. Get them asking each other good questions. Challenge them to think about the positive and negatives of committing to meet for one year. Get them thinking about fulfilling Matthew 28:18-20. Suggest to your follower to read the "Real-Life Discipleship: An Ordinary Man's Guide To Disciplemaking" book. You may even consider buying him his own copy!

Example questions:
How do you guys feel about this?
What are you most excited about?
What questions do you have for me?
How can I be praying for both of you?
Do you think God is using both of you right now to advance his kingdom?

Notes from your time together:

WATCH ME AS I LEAD
Mark 6:7-12

Bible verses to reflect on when discussing where you are headed:
Matthew 28:18-20, Matthew 5:14-16, Luke 14:27, Ephesians 4:11-17,
Luke 9:23, Luke 6:40, 1 Corinthians 11:1

Things to center your time around:
The idea this week is for you just to be around your follower and his new disciple. Ensure both of them are committed and spend your time today listening. Allow your follower to lead!

Example questions:
You should have very little to say this week. The past year has been spent building up and speaking into the life of your follower. This week just be the wind beneath his wings, allowing him to fly.

Notes from your time together:

Tom Cheshire

Tom is married to his helper and wonderful wife, Jan Cheshire. Tom and Jan have two adult daughters Amelia and Lindleigh and son-in-law Logan.

Tom served in the USMC 1976-1980 where he fell in love with aviation and a career in corporate aviation from 1980 until 2002. Tom has been in men's ministry really all his life but has been in leadership in both his church as an elder and in the community for the last 20 years.

Tom's passion for discipleship is born out of godly men investing in him to grow in Christ. Tom is also active in his church (Delta Church) as one of the Elders, with oversight of discipleship as one of his responsibilities. Tom has been an active member of the National Coalition of Men's Ministry (NCMM) since 2002, as well as one of the charter members of the national conference ministry, Iron Sharpens Iron (ISI). In 2007 Tom founded his second non-profit, Relevant Practical Ministry for Men (RPM) which is a servant ministry to the local church, to see her men maturing in Christ. RPM does that by investing in pastors and leaders to help them develop or strengthen a robust discipleship culture.

Tom Gensler

Tom and his beautiful wife Lisa have been married since 2004 and are in love with Jesus and each other. They have five children Ruby, Moses, Gabriel, Shiloh & Selah, and they reside in Decatur, IL.

Tom is a graduate from the University of Illinois in Springfield with a Bachelor of Arts in Management. He served six years as an Infantryman in the Illinois Army National Guard and spent 14 years working in the automotive industry gaining experience in every area of an auto dealership concluding with five years managing a multi-million-dollar service department with a multi-line dealership.

Tom has accumulated credit hours with Lincoln Christian Seminary and Urbana Theological Seminary in pursuit of a Masters of Divinity Degree. He has also acquired an Advanced Christian Life Coaching Certificate and has completed a Church Planting and Leadership Course through Dove Christian Fellowship International (DCFI).

As a result of their own marriage struggles, the Gensler family is passionate about men understanding all that God intended for them, and in-turn loves seeing marriages and families thrive. Tom & Lisa started volunteering with RPM in 2007 and joined the full-time staff as missionaries in Feb of 2013.